RAIN FOREST WILDLIFE

Consultant: William A. Xanten
Illustrators: Barbara Gibson, Stuart Armstrong

Published by
The National Geographic Society
John M. Fahey, Jr., President and Chief Executive Officer
Gilbert M. Grosvenor, Chairman of the Board
Nina D. Hoffman, President, Books and School Publishing

Staff for this Book
Barbara Brownell, Director of Continuities
Marianne R. Koszorus, Director of Layout and Design
Toni Eugene, Editor
Alexandra Littlehales, Art Director
Marfé Ferguson Delano, Writer-Researcher
Susan V. Kelly, Illustrations Editor
Melissa Hunsiker, Assistant Editor
Sharon Kocsis Berry, Illustrations Assistant
Mark A. Caraluzzi, Vice President, Sales and Marketing
Heidi Vincent, Director, Direct Marketing
Vincent P. Ryan, Manufacturing Manager
Lewis R. Bassford, Production Project Manager

Visit our Web site at www.nationalgeographic.com

Library of Congress Catalog Card Number: 2001 - 130281
ISBN: 0-7922-6594-7

Color separations by Quad Graphics, Martinsburg, West Virginia
Printed in Mexico by R.R. Donnelley & Sons Company

RAIN FOREST WILDLIFE

MARFÉ FERGUSON DELANO

All photographs supplied by Animals Animals/Earth Scenes

NATIONAL
GEOGRAPHIC
SOCIETY

INTRODUCTION

Rain forests contain more different kinds of animals than any other habitat on Earth. A rain forest is an area of thick forest where at least four inches of rain falls each month.

Most of the world's rain forests are found in the tropics, the area north and south of the Equator that is warm all year. Trees there are mainly evergreens with wide leaves.

But not all rain forests are tropical. Some, called temperate rain forests, grow in cooler parts of the world, such as North America's Pacific Northwest region. Temperate rain forests are made up of needle-leaved evergreen trees, such as firs, spruces, and cedars.

In this book you will meet 34 different animals that live in rain forests around the world. Sadly, many of these creatures are in danger of becoming extinct. Their habitats are being destroyed as people clear rain forest lands for farming and logging.

HOW TO USE THIS BOOK

The animals in this book are arranged according to the layer of the rain forest in which they spend much of their time: forest floor, understory, or canopy. These layers are discussed on page 6. Within each layer, animals are organized by type. Birds are grouped together, mammals are together, and so on. Each type of creature is presented from smallest to largest.

Each spread helps identify one animal and tells about its size, color, and behavior. A shaded map shows where to find each creature. The "Field Notes" entry gives an additional fact about it. Look up words you don't know in the Glossary on page 76.

FOREST LAYERS

Rain forests can be divided into three different layers: the forest floor, the understory, and the canopy.

The forest floor is the ground level. It is covered with a tangle of roots, fallen leaves, and low-growing plants. Above the forest floor is the understory, which contains bushes and small trees. The canopy, which consists of the leaves and branches of the tallest trees, is the top layer of a rain forest.

Besides trees and bushes, a variety of other plants grow in rain forests. Thick vines climb up tree trunks, twisting and winding their way through the treetops. Orchids, ferns, and mosses grow on the bark of canopy trees. These plants, which get water and nutrients from the air and rain, are called epiphytes (EP-uh-fights). Bromeliads (bro-ME-lee-ads) are cup-shaped epiphytes that collect water. Many canopy-dwelling creatures drink from these treetop pools, and some frogs and insects lay their eggs in them.

canopy

understory

forest floor

ARMY ANT

 Like soldiers on the move, army ants march in columns across the forest floor. Tiny but ferocious hunters, they devour everything in their path, from other insects to lizards to small mammals.

WHERE TO FIND:

SOUTH AMERICA

Army ants can be found throughout much of Central and South America.

WHAT TO LOOK FOR:

✳ **SIZE**
Army ants are ¹/₂ to 1 inch long.

✳ **COLOR**
Most are yellowish or reddish brown.

✳ **BEHAVIOR**
Army ants rest in temporary nests, which they make by linking their bodies together. The queen lays her eggs at the center of the nest.

✳ **MORE**
A colony, or group, of army ants can have more than a million members.

Army ants have large, razor-sharp jaws, which they use to seize prey and tear it to bits.

GIANT MILLIPEDE

 Giant millipedes are a lot longer than the ordinary millipedes found around the world, and they also have more legs. The biggest giant millipede can have up to 375 pairs of legs.

FIELD NOTES

When threatened, a giant millipede rolls up into a tight spiral, with its head in the center.

WHAT TO LOOK FOR:

✳ SIZE
Giant millipedes can be 12 inches or longer and as thick as a person's finger.

✳ COLOR
They are usually dark brown or black. Some are red.

✳ BEHAVIOR
Females lay their eggs in the ground or in a nest they build from soil.

✳ MORE
Giant millipedes can live to be seven years of age.

Like a shiny suit of armor, a hard outer skeleton helps protect the millipede's body.

POISON-DART FROG

 Jewel-like skin colors make poison-dart frogs lovely to look at. But these amphibians can be deadly. Their skin produces a poison powerful enough to kill predators.

SOUTH AMERICA

WHERE TO FIND:
Many different kinds of poison-dart frogs live in Central America and northern South America.

WHAT TO LOOK FOR:

✳ **SIZE**
They are ½ to 2 inches long.

✳ **COLOR**
They can be bright blue, red, yellow, or green. Many have black patches.

✳ **BEHAVIOR**
Poison-dart frogs lay their eggs on land and guard them until they hatch.

✳ **MORE**
Parent frogs load newly hatched tadpoles on their backs and carry them to water to continue developing.

The poison-dart frog's bright colors warn predators, such as birds, to stay away.

GABOON VIPER

This big snake is an ambush expert. It lurks unseen among fallen leaves and waits for a rat or other prey to come along. Then this reptile strikes fast, sinking deadly fangs into its victim.

AFRICA

WHERE TO FIND:
The gaboon viper lives on the ground in the rain forests of western and central Africa.

WHAT TO LOOK FOR:

✳ SIZE
It can grow to more than 6 feet in length and can weigh up to 18 pounds.

✳ COLOR
It has a geometric pattern of gray, beige, white, and purple.

✳ BEHAVIOR
When alarmed, the gaboon viper puffs up its body and hisses.

✳ MORE
Gaboon vipers give birth to live young, with up to 60 in a litter.

The gaboon viper's colors help it blend in with dead leaves on the forest floor.

15

NORTH AMERICAN PORCUPINE

 Unlike its cousins in Africa and Asia, which live on the ground, this porcupine is also at home in trees. Curved claws help the mammal climb.

WHERE TO FIND:
North American porcupines live in temperate rain forests and other forested areas in North America.

NORTH AMERICA

WHAT TO LOOK FOR:

✳ SIZE
They measure about three feet long.

✳ COLOR
They have dark brown or black fur. Their spines, called quills, can be yellow, white, brown, or black.

✳ BEHAVIOR
When threatened, a porcupine raises and spreads out its quills, which usually lie flat against its body.

✳ MORE
Porcupines eat bark and leaves.

The porcupine's face and belly are not protected by quills.

Like barbs on a fishhook, scales on a porcupine's quills catch tightly in an attacker's body.

TREE PANGOLIN

 A tree pangolin looks like a pinecone with legs. Pangolins crawl around the ground at night searching for termite and ant nests. They spend much of the day resting in trees.

FIELD NOTES

When a leopard or other enemy comes near, the pangolin curls its body into a tight, scaly ball.

The tree pangolin uses its long tongue to lap up water as well as to probe ant and termite nests.

WHERE TO FIND:

AFRICA

Tree pangolins live in African rain forests. Other kinds of pangolins live in African deserts and in Asia.

WHAT TO LOOK FOR:

✳ **SIZE**
Tree pangolins are about three feet long, including the tail.

✳ **COLOR**
They are covered with hard, brownish gray scales that have sharp edges.

✳ **BEHAVIOR**
They use their strong tails to hold on as they move around in trees.

✳ **MORE**
To shield her young, a mother pangolin curls herself around its body.

MANDRILL

The bright colors on a male mandrill's face also appear on its rump. The markings help the monkey's family group follow it through the jungle.

AFRICA

WHERE TO FIND:

Mandrills live on the ground and in low tree branches in the rain forests of central Africa.

WHAT TO LOOK FOR:

✳ SIZE
Male mandrills can measure nearly three feet long. Females are smaller.

✳ COLOR
Mandrills have grayish brown fur. Males have blue and red faces.

✳ BEHAVIOR
They usually live in family groups of 15 to 20; each group has one adult male.

✳ MORE
Mandrills look under stones for insects to eat. They also feed on fruit and nuts.

To get around on the ground, mandrills walk on all fours, using their fingers as toes.

When a mother mandrill travels or looks for food, she carries along her young, which clings to her belly.

JAGUAR

 Largest predator in American rain forests, the jaguar creeps up on its prey, then pounces. Its powerful jaws can crack the skulls of its victims, which include mammals, birds, reptiles, and fish.

NORTH AMERICA

SOUTH AMERICA

WHERE TO FIND:
Jaguars prowl rain forests, riverbanks, and other swampy places in Central and South America.

WHAT TO LOOK FOR:

✳ SIZE
Jaguars are seven to eight feet long, including a two-foot tail.

✳ COLOR
Their fur is usually golden, with rings of small black dots called rosettes.

✳ BEHAVIOR
Except during mating time, jaguars tend to live alone.

✳ MORE
A jaguar's roar sounds like a loud bark or cough. The cats roar to attract mates.

The jaguar's spotted coat helps it blend in with the light and shade of the rain forest. Jaguars are heavier than their African cousins, leopards.

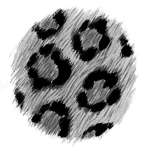

leopard

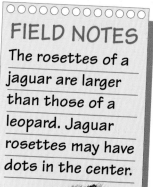

jaguar

BRAZILIAN TAPIR

 To cool off during the heat of midday, Brazilian tapirs wallow in mud. These mud baths also help the big mammals rid themselves of ticks.

WHERE TO FIND:
The Brazilian tapir is one of three kinds of tapirs found in rain forests of Central and South America.

SOUTH AMERICA

WHAT TO LOOK FOR:

✳ **SIZE**
Brazilian tapirs are 6 to 7 feet long and weigh about 500 pounds.

✳ **COLOR**
They are black or grayish brown, with short, bristly fur.

✳ **BEHAVIOR**
Tapirs usually run away when they are threatened, but if necessary they will defend themselves by biting.

✳ **MORE**
Jaguars sometimes prey on tapirs.

Like all tapirs, the Brazilian tapir has a small trunk, short legs, and a long, massive body. It is a good runner and swimmer.

FIELD NOTES

Tapirs often dive underwater to munch on swamp grass. They also eat leaves, buds, twigs, and fruit.

PACIFIC TREE FROG

 Chances are you've heard this frog's "ribbet, ribbet." Its voice is so loud and froggy that it is often recorded for use in movie and television sound tracks.

WHERE TO FIND:
The Pacific tree frog lives in temperate rain forests and other moist places in western North America.

NORTH AMERICA

WHAT TO LOOK FOR:

✳ **SIZE**
Pacific tree frogs range in size from ³/₄ to 2 inches long.

✳ **COLOR**
They are green, tan, brown, or black.

✳ **BEHAVIOR**
During breeding season, male frogs gather in groups called choruses and call together to attract females.

✳ **MORE**
The frogs dwell on low-growing plants near water and feed on insects.

Most tree frogs have a dark stripe that runs through the eye area.

FIELD NOTES

Powerful hind legs make tree frogs good jumpers. They leap to escape predators, such as snakes.

CHAMELEON

 Chameleons are famous for their ability to change the color and pattern of their skin. Such changes are triggered by variations in sunlight or temperature, or when the lizard senses a threat.

WHERE TO FIND:
Many different kinds of chameleons can be found in the rain forests of Africa, Madagascar, and India.

WHAT TO LOOK FOR:

✳ SIZE
Chameleons range in length from less than an inch to more than 16 inches.

✳ COLOR
They are usually green or brown.

✳ BEHAVIOR
They can move each eye separately from the other, so they can look in opposite directions at the same time.

✳ MORE
Most kinds of chameleons lay eggs, but some give birth to live young.

The chameleon shoots out its sticky tongue to grab insects. Its tongue can be as long as its body.

The chameleon's body is flattened. Its narrow shape helps it balance and move on slender branches.

GREEN IGUANA

The green iguana is a plant-eating lizard that often sunbathes on tree branches overhanging rivers. If danger approaches, the creature drops into the water and swims away.

FIELD NOTES

Baby iguanas hatch from tough, leathery eggs laid in sand. They are about eight inches long at birth.

A crest of tooth-like scales runs along the iguana's back and tail.

WHERE TO FIND:

Also called the common iguana, the green iguana lives in rain forested areas of Central and South America.

WHAT TO LOOK FOR:

✷ SIZE
Green iguanas grow to be 6¹/₂ feet long.

✷ COLOR
They are green or bluish green. Males may have orange markings.

✷ BEHAVIOR
If unable to escape from danger, green iguanas bite to protect themselves.

✷ MORE
Some people of the rain forest hunt iguanas for their meat and eggs.

EYELASH VIPER

 This poisonous snake loops itself around branches, flowers, or fruit and waits for prey to draw near. Heat-sensing organs on the reptile's head help it detect prey.

WHERE TO FIND:

NORTH AMERICA

SOUTH AMERICA

The eyelash viper can be found in rain forests from southern Mexico to northern South America.

WHAT TO LOOK FOR:

✳ SIZE
An eyelash viper is 18 to 30 inches in length.

✳ COLOR
It comes in a variety of colors, including yellow, green, and brown.

✳ BEHAVIOR
Females give birth to a dozen or more live young.

✳ MORE
The snake's venomous bite is powerful enough to kill a human being.

The eyelash viper gets its name from the large, pointed scales above its eyes that look like eyelashes.

Lured by the snake's color, hummingbirds are frequent victims of yellow eyelash vipers.

HOATZIN

The hoatzin (WAT-seen) takes days to digest the leaves it eats. The food, stored in the bird's throat, produces an odor that gives it another name, "stink bird."

The hoatzin has a large body and a small head crowned by spiky feathers.

WHERE TO FIND:

SOUTH AMERICA

The hoatzin lives along thickly forested riverbanks and lake shores in northern South America.

WHAT TO LOOK FOR:

✳ SIZE
The hoatzin is about two feet long.

✳ COLOR
It has black, white, and brown feathers and a blue head.

✳ BEHAVIOR
Hoatzins build nests in branches over water. Chicks flee danger by jumping into the water and swimming away.

✳ MORE
Once chicks learn to fly, they soon shed the claws on their wings.

FIELD NOTES

Hoatzin chicks have foot-like claws on their wings, which help them climb through branches.

VAMPIRE BAT

Each night, vampire bats leave their daytime sleeping place to search for their evening meal. The mouse-size mammals feed on the blood of cattle, chickens, donkeys, and deer. They rarely bite humans.

FIELD NOTES

With razor-sharp teeth, the vampire bat makes a tiny cut in its victim's skin, then licks up the blood.

The vampire bat uses its nose, which detects heat as well as odors, to help it find prey.

NORTH
AMERICA

SOUTH
AMERICA

WHERE TO FIND:
Vampire bats roost in
caves and hollow trees
throughout much of
Central and South America.

WHAT TO LOOK FOR:

✳ SIZE
Vampire bats are three to four inches
long and weigh about one ounce.

✳ COLOR
They are usually dark grayish brown.

✳ BEHAVIOR
When they return to their roost,
vampire bats will throw up blood to
share with those that did not find food.

✳ MORE
Vampire bats must drink 50 percent of
their body weight in blood each night.

FLYING FOX

 The expression "blind as a bat" does not apply to flying foxes. These large bats have keen night vision, which helps them find their way to and from the fruit trees on which they feed.

WHERE TO FIND:

ASIA

There are many kinds of flying foxes. The largest live in rain forests and swamps of India and Southeast Asia.

WHAT TO LOOK FOR:

✳ SIZE
The biggest flying foxes have 16-inch-long bodies and 6-foot wingspans.

✳ COLOR
Most flying foxes are brown.

✳ BEHAVIOR
At dusk, flying foxes leave their roosts and fly to fruit trees. They may travel 30 miles or more in search of food.

✳ MORE
They return to their roosts before dawn, clean their wings, and settle to sleep.

The flying fox owes its name to its fox-like snout and ears. During the day, it rests upside down in a tree, hanging by its feet.

FIELD NOTES

Flying foxes give birth to one young. Totally helpless, it spends its first weeks clinging to its mother's body.

TREE KANGAROO

 Tree kangaroos are pouched mammals, or marsupials. They climb and leap from tree to tree at night, feeding on leaves and fruit. If startled, they may jump 60 feet from a tree branch to the ground.

WHERE TO FIND:

NEW GUINEA

AUSTRALIA

Tree kangaroos are at home only in the rain forests of New Guinea and the northern tip of Australia.

WHAT TO LOOK FOR:

✳ SIZE
A tree kangaroo ranges from four to six feet in length, including its tail. Its tail can be as long as the body.

✳ COLOR
The animals are brown or gray.

✳ BEHAVIOR
Tree kangaroo babies, or joeys, stay in their mother's pouch for up to one year.

✳ MORE
Tree kangaroos have long, curved claws, which help them grip branches.

A tree kangaroo spends much of its day curled up on a branch, resting.

FIELD NOTES

Tree kangaroos have shorter back legs and stronger front legs than the gray kangaroo, a ground dweller.

MORPHO BUTTERFLY

So beautiful are the shiny blue wings of male morpho butterflies that they were once used in necklaces and other jewelry. Female morphos are less colorful.

FIELD NOTES

Circular markings called eyespots decorate the brown underside of a morpho butterfly's wings.

A black border with white and red dots edges the morpho's blue wings.

SOUTH AMERICA

WHAT TO LOOK FOR:

✳ SIZE
Morpho butterflies have wingspans of three to six inches.

✳ COLOR
The insects are a bright metallic blue.

✳ BEHAVIOR
They often fly close to the forest floor, where they are attracted to the juices of fallen fruit.

✳ MORE
Morpho young, or caterpillars, feed on grasses, bamboo, and other plants.

RED-EYED TREE FROG

Leaping like an acrobat from branch to branch, these frogs hunt for insects in treetops at night. Large eyes help this nocturnal frog spot prey in the dark.

WHERE TO FIND:
The red-eyed tree frog spends most of its life in trees in forests of Mexico and Central America.

NORTH AMERICA

SOUTH AMERICA

WHAT TO LOOK FOR:

✳ **SIZE**
These frogs are about three inches long.

✳ **COLOR**
They are bright green, with blue and yellow stripes on their sides.

✳ **BEHAVIOR**
Females lay eggs on a leaf hanging over water. When the tadpoles hatch, they fall off the leaf into the water.

✳ **MORE**
After tadpoles develop into frogs, they leave the water and climb into trees.

Sticky toe pads that work like suction cups help tree frogs cling to twigs and leaves.

EMERALD TREE BOA

Looped around a high branch, this snake spends the night hanging around. When a bird or bat passes by, the boa lunges, grabbing it with sharp teeth.

FIELD NOTES

Emerald tree boas are brick red at birth. They turn green, usually by the time they are three feet long.

White markings break up the snake's outline in the daytime and help it blend in with the light-dappled leaves of the forest canopy.

WHERE TO FIND:

The emerald tree boa lives in South America. About 60 kinds of boas are found in warm regions of the world.

WHAT TO LOOK FOR:

✳ SIZE
The emerald tree boa measures 6½ feet in length.

✳ COLOR
It is bright green, with white patches along its back.

✳ BEHAVIOR
Like all boas, this snake kills prey by squeezing it until it cannot breathe. Then it swallows its victim headfirst.

✳ MORE
Females give birth to live young.

AFRICAN GRAY PARROT

 In the wild, African gray parrots screech, twitter, and whistle to each other. In captivity, they can learn to copy hundreds of human words.

AFRICA

WHERE TO FIND:
The African gray parrot lives and nests in trees in the rain forests of central Africa.

WHAT TO LOOK FOR:

✳ SIZE
The African gray parrot is about one foot long.

✳ COLOR
It is light gray with a bright red tail.

✳ BEHAVIOR
Like all parrots, it uses its thick, hooked beak to crack the seeds and nuts on which it feeds.

✳ MORE
It sometimes flies down to the ground to search for food.

African gray parrots have a patch of bare skin around their eyes. Males and females look alike.

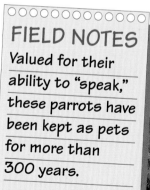

FIELD NOTES
Valued for their ability to "speak," these parrots have been kept as pets for more than 300 years.

TOUCAN

 Toucans make a lot of noise, but not many people would call it singing. These colorful canopy dwellers bark, croak, and make noises that sound like bugles.

WHERE TO FIND:
More than 30 kinds of toucans make their homes in the rain forests of South America.

WHAT TO LOOK FOR:

✳ SIZE
Toucans are about two feet long.

✳ COLOR
They are mostly black, with a white throat and a rainbow-colored beak.

✳ BEHAVIOR
Toucans sometimes steal eggs from the nests of other birds and eat them.

✳ MORE
The large size and bright colors of the toucan's beak help it attract mates and scare away enemies.

Toucans build their nests in holes they find in trees. Their big beaks look heavy, but weigh little because they are hollow.

BIRD OF PARADISE

CANOPY

Male birds of paradise are the show-offs of the bird world. To attract a mate, they perch on a branch, puff out their gorgeous feathers, and call out loudly for attention.

WHERE TO FIND:

NEW GUINEA

AUSTRALIA

About 40 kinds of birds of paradise are found in the rain forests of New Guinea and northern Australia.

WHAT TO LOOK FOR:

✳ **SIZE**
Birds of paradise range in length from about one foot to more than three feet.

✳ **COLOR**
They come in a variety of colors, including vivid red, blue, and yellow.

✳ **BEHAVIOR**
Females usually nest and raise their young without help from their mates.

✳ **MORE**
Females tend to be dull in color. They have no tail plumes.

Males, such as this king bird of paradise, boast two long tail plumes, which may have coiled feathers at the end.

SCARLET MACAW

 Named for its brilliant red color, this large parrot often eats bitter fruits that other creatures avoid. It also eats clay from riverbanks, which may help it digest the bitter food.

WHERE TO FIND:
Scarlet macaws live high in trees on the edge of rain forests in Central and South America.

SOUTH AMERICA

WHAT TO LOOK FOR:

✳ SIZE
The scarlet macaw measures about three feet long.

✳ COLOR
It is red with bright yellow, green, and blue feathers on its wings.

✳ BEHAVIOR
Scarlet macaws mate for life and raise one or two young at a time.

✳ MORE
When alarmed, these birds screech loudly and fly away.

Like all parrots, macaws have feet with two toes pointing forward and two pointing backward. This gives them a good grip.

RHINOCEROS HORNBILL

A female hornbill lays her eggs inside a tree hole she and her mate seal with mud. She stays inside the hideaway and cares for the chicks when they hatch.

FIELD NOTES

The male brings his mate about 30 meals a day, passing them to her through a slit in the mud seal.

This bird is named for the huge, horn-like growth on top of its beak.

ASIA

AUSTRALIA

WHERE TO FIND:
The rhinoceros hornbill lives in Southeast Asia. Other kinds of hornbills live in African rain forests.

WHAT TO LOOK FOR:

✳ SIZE
The rhinoceros hornbill measures 49 inches long.

✳ COLOR
It is black with a white rump and tail.

✳ BEHAVIOR
When the chicks are a few weeks old, the female pecks her way out of the nest and helps the male collect food for them.

✳ MORE
Rhinoceros hornbills eat mostly fruit and sometimes the young of other birds.

SUGAR GLIDER

The sugar glider sails through the night air from tree to tree, feeding on nectar and other sweet foods. Like the tree kangaroo, it is a marsupial, or pouched animal.

FIELD NOTES

Stretching out flaps of skin between its arms and legs, a glider can travel 150 feet in a single leap.

WHERE TO FIND:
Sugar gliders live in rain forests and other wooded areas in parts of New Guinea and Australia.

WHAT TO LOOK FOR:

✳ SIZE
The sugar glider grows 11 to 15 inches long, including the tail.

✳ COLOR
It is gray with a white underside. A dark stripe runs down its back.

✳ BEHAVIOR
Tiny as a grain of rice, a newborn sugar glider crawls into its mother's pouch, where it nurses and grows.

✳ MORE
In flight, the glider steers with its tail.

After a flight, the sugar glider lands on all four feet with its claws extended.

59

TARSIER

At sunset, tarsiers (TAR-see-urz) wake up and start hunting for insects and lizards. Propelled by strong hind legs, these pint-size kin of monkeys leap like tree frogs from branch to branch.

WHERE TO FIND:
Tarsiers are found in trees and on bamboo plants in Indonesia and the Philippines.

WHAT TO LOOK FOR:

✳ **SIZE**
Tarsiers are three to six inches long, not including the tail, which can be twice that long.

✳ **COLOR**
They are grayish or brown in color.

✳ **BEHAVIOR**
Tarsiers pounce on their prey, snatch it up with their long fingers, then bite it.

✳ **MORE**
Like an owl, the tarsier can rotate its head so that it can see behind itself.

Enormous eyes and sensitive ears help the tarsier see and hear small prey at night.

GOLDEN LION TAMARIN

 Golden lion tamarins are good fathers. These monkeys not only help carry and feed their offspring but also play with them and pick fleas out of their fur.

WHERE TO FIND:
The tree-dwelling golden lion tamarin is native to rain forests near the southern coast of Brazil.

SOUTH AMERICA

WHAT TO LOOK FOR:

✳ **SIZE**
The golden lion tamarin is about 20 to 30 inches long, including its long tail.

✳ **COLOR**
It is covered with long, silky golden yellow or reddish gold fur.

✳ **BEHAVIOR**
Tamarins communicate by trilling, clucking, whistling, and whining.

✳ **MORE**
By day, they search the trees for fruit, insects, lizards, and birds' eggs to eat.

FIELD NOTES

At night, the tamarin curls up in a vine, a tree hole, or a treetop plant called an epiphyte to sleep.

The lion-like mane covering its head and shoulders gives this small, acrobatic monkey its name.

MARTEN

Members of the weasel family, martens scurry along branches chasing squirrels and other prey. They often hide their kill and eat it later.

FIELD NOTES

A large kind of marten called a fisher kills a porcupine by biting repeatedly at its face.

Martens are also at home on the ground, where fallen trees provide hiding places from predators such as bobcats and owls.

WHAT TO LOOK FOR:

✳ SIZE
Martens range in length from about 20 to 40 inches, including their bushy tail.

✳ COLOR
They are dark brown, with a paler face and throat.

✳ BEHAVIOR
They raise their young in dens in hollow trees.

✳ MORE
Martens have long been hunted for their luxurious fur, used to make coats.

RING-TAILED LEMUR

 Ring-tailed lemurs live in groups of about 15. At night, they all share the same sleeping tree. During the day, they often spend time on the ground.

WHERE TO FIND:
The ring-tailed lemur is one of about 55 kinds of lemurs found on Madagascar and nearby islands off Africa.

AFRICA

WHAT TO LOOK FOR:

✳ **SIZE**
The ring-tailed lemur is about 40 inches long, including its 2-foot tail.

✳ **COLOR**
It is brownish gray, with a black-and-white striped tail.

✳ **BEHAVIOR**
To communicate, this monkey relative purrs, howls, screams, and hoots.

✳ **MORE**
Ring-tailed lemurs eat fruit, flowers, leaves, and other plant parts.

A young lemur rides on its mother's back. It will depend on her until it is five months old.

THREE-TOED SLOTH

The word "sloth" means laziness, and this slow-moving mammal deserves its name. Hanging upside down in treetops, it sleeps 15 hours or more each day.

Tiny organisms called algae live in the three-toed sloth's coat, giving it a greenish tint that makes the animal hard to see in the trees.

A young sloth clings tightly to its mother's fur until it goes off on its own at the age of nine months.

SOUTH AMERICA

WHERE TO FIND:

The three-toed sloth and its cousin, the two-toed sloth, live in Central and South America.

WHAT TO LOOK FOR:

✱ **SIZE**
It measures 20 to 25 inches long.

✱ **COLOR**
Its fur is grayish brown.

✱ **BEHAVIOR**
At night, the sloth travels through the trees, holding on to branches with hook-like claws and feeding on leaves.

✱ **MORE**
The sloth's huge claws make walking impossible. It moves on the ground by dragging itself along.

TAMANDUA

 Tamanduas (tuh-MAN-duh-wuz) climb through trees hunting for ant or termite nests. They rip a nest open, flick their long, sticky tongue inside, and pull it out covered with insects.

WHERE TO FIND:
The tamandua is one of several kinds of anteaters that live in Central and South America.

SOUTH AMERICA

WHAT TO LOOK FOR:

✳ SIZE
Tamanduas grow about four feet long, including a strong, two-foot tail.

✳ COLOR
They are yellowish, brown, or black, and may have dark markings.

✳ BEHAVIOR
Tamandua females carry their young on their backs.

✳ MORE
During the day, tamanduas curl up in a tree fork and sleep.

A frightened tamandua rises on its hind legs and spreads its paws, ready to slash with razor-sharp claws.

The tamandua sniffs for food with its long, slender snout.

HOWLER MONKEY

Every morning when they wake up, these monkeys let loose with the earsplitting howls that give them their name. They roar again in the evening before settling down to sleep.

SOUTH AMERICA

WHERE TO FIND:
Nine kinds of howler monkeys make their homes in rain forests in Central and South America.

WHAT TO LOOK FOR:

✷ SIZE
Howler monkeys are four to eight feet long, half of which is tail.

✷ COLOR
Most kinds of howlers are yellowish brown, reddish brown, or black.

✷ BEHAVIOR
A howler monkey uses its strong tail to help it swing from limb to limb.

✷ MORE
The cry made by howler monkeys can be heard two miles away.

An enlarged throat helps this monkey create its cry. Males have bigger throats and louder voices than females.

FIELD NOTES
Howlers live in groups of 3 to 20 animals. They howl to warn other groups to keep their distance.

ORANGUTAN

 Orangutans are the largest of all tree-dwelling mammals. Moving arm over arm through the branches, the heavy apes search for wild figs and other fruit.

Pale when the ape is young, the face of an orangutan darkens as it ages.

ASIA

AUSTRALIA

WHERE TO FIND:
Orangutans are found only in the forests of the islands of Borneo and Sumatra in Indonesia.

WHAT TO LOOK FOR:

✳ **SIZE**
Orangutans grow to be four to five feet tall. Males weigh about 155 pounds, females weigh about 80.

✳ **COLOR**
They have shaggy, orange-brown fur.

✳ **BEHAVIOR**
In heavy rains, orangutans sometimes use a large leaf as an umbrella.

✳ **MORE**
Mothers and young stay together for about six years.

FIELD NOTES
Orangutans learn early in life to use leafy branches to build the treetop nests they sleep in every night.

GLOSSARY

amphibian A cold-blooded animal, such as a frog, that has moist skin without scales and spends part of its life in water.

evergreens Trees that bear leaves all year, shedding a small number continuously.

eyespots Bold, circular markings on an insect that resemble large eyes. They may help scare off enemies.

habitat The place where an animal or plant is normally found.

mammal A warm-blooded animal, usually with hair or fur, that feeds its young on milk from the mother's body.

marsupial A mammal that is underdeveloped at birth and grows inside its mother's pouch, where it nurses until it can survive outside her body.

mate When an adult male and female come together to produce young.

nectar The sugary liquid made in a flower that attracts insects and other animals that spread the flower's pollen.

nocturnal Active at night.

predator An animal that hunts and kills other animals for food.

prey An animal hunted for food.

reptile A cold-blooded animal that has scaly or leathery skin and usually lays eggs. Lizards and snakes are reptiles.

roost A tree or other place where birds or other animals rest or sleep, either alone or in groups.

venom A poisonous substance that is formed and transmitted by some animals, such as snakes and bees, usually by biting or stinging.

INDEX OF
RAIN FOREST
WILDLIFE